WORDSONGS

BY

C. STEVEN BLUE

The Wordsongs Series

Book 1

WORDSONGS

ISBN 0-9635499-5-2
ISBN13 978-0-9635499-5-2

Third edition (revised): 2016
Trade paperback

First edition: 1992
Hand-made edition: 1994
Revised hand-made edition: 2010 - 2012
Second edition (revised): 2016

Published by:

>—*ARROWCLOUD*—>
PRESS

For more information go to www.wordsongs.com

Album Contents:

Dedication...

For my children: Anthony, Justin and Tara
Sometimes you were all that kept me going

I would like to thank my Copy Editors:

Paulette Schreiner
Michele Graf
Katharine Valentino

...Quotation...

"Each heart . . . a different answer
Each soul . . . a different name
Life's images are many
But the source remains the same"

The Fool*

*From an inscription painted on the side of the Aquarius Theatre,
Hollywood, CA (circa 1968)

...Introduction...

WORDSONGS, the first album in The Wordsongs Series, has as its theme, the story of a young man living in the inner city who dreams of freedom and true love.

Follow his journey as he struggles with the concept of freedom, finds then loses his first love and discovers himself in the process. Will he find love again? The answer is inside—in the first and original **WORDSONGS**.

The Wordsongs Series

Each book in this series contains 20 pieces designed to be similar in scope to a music record album, with side one and side two, but instead of songs it is comprised of a style of poems called wordsongs. Each book is a concept album, with a general theme running through it, told in verse format.

Wordsongs are the original creation of C. Steven Blue, who also created a definition for this concept:

word'song, n. [AS. wordsong.]
1. a poem that is like a song or could be a song
2. verses that tell a story in song-like rhythm, often with a refrain
3. a song that you read

...Inspiration

. . . If music speaks, do words sing?

Some music speaks to your senses without words.
Wordsongs sing to your senses without music.
Wordsongs speak to your inner rhythms.

The 20 wordsongs in this album tell a story.
Any music that they sing to you . . .
must come from the inner ear of your own imagination;
the musical tapestry of your mind.

Turn the pages and listen . . .
to these words.

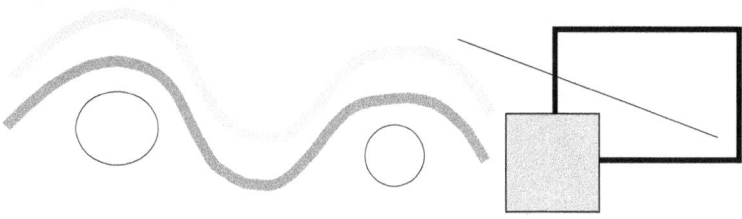

Side One...

21ˢᵗ Century Madness

Freedom
Knock on my door
What's more
Find me
Remind me how it used to be
Freedom

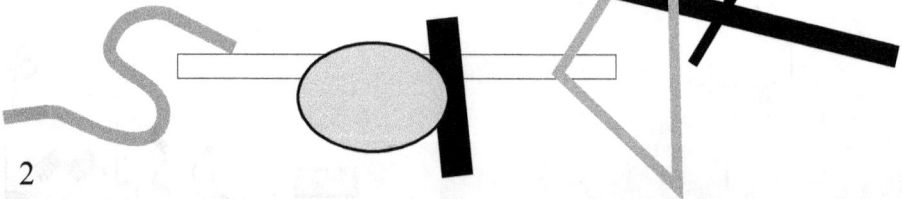

Where do I go
To breathe
What can I do
To get away
From the mania and the sadness
Of this man-made . . . movie
Becoming 21ˢᵗ century madness

Get down on your front lawn
If you have one
Stare up at the stars
If you can see any
Remember a more innocent time
If the bugs and city noises
Don't distract your mind too much

Freedom
Knock on my door
What's more
Find me
Remind me how it used to be
Freedom

Moments of peace and contentment
Are far too few
Fulfillment
It's a hazy view
Is it fog
Or is it smog
I'm trying to see through

Where do I go
To breathe
What can I do
To get away
From the mania and the sadness
Of this man-made . . . movie
Becoming 21st century madness

Freedom
Knock on my door
What's more
Find me
Remind me how it used to be
Freedom

Another Night In The City

Red light/blue light
Swerving down
Six lanes of busy freeway
To smooth control
The traffic flow
For safety . . . down the way

A man stands by the roadside
His head bowed down
To the ground
Arms behind him
Hand-cuffed tight
I can almost feel
His loneliness bound

Another night in the city
The many things I see
A thousand lonely people
Pass me by
Another night on the freeway
The way it always seems to be
So many lonely people
Wonder why

Hurry people
On your way
Don't take the time to know
That even in the city
Flowers grow

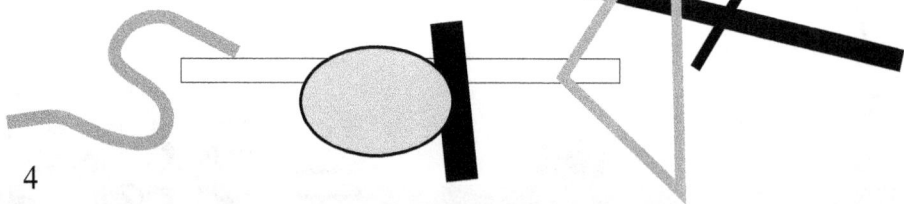

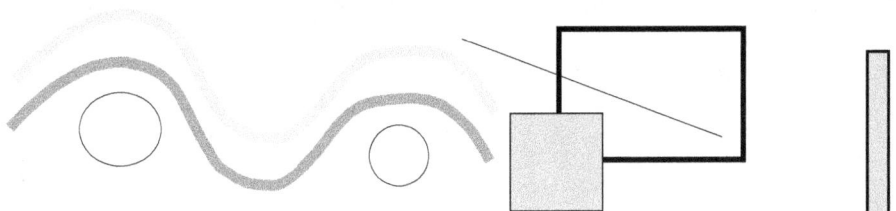

Don't take the time to see
The sunset by the sea
The skyline
Or the moon that shines above me

Red light/blue light
Swerving down
Six lanes of busy freeway
Smooth control
The traffic flow
For safety . . . down the way

Lonely girl on a freeway bridge
Looks like she's gonna jump
. . . Into the air
People gather
While the next exit down
A helicopter circles
With spotlight glare

Another night in the city
The many things I see
A thousand lonely people
Pass me by
Another night on the freeway
The way it always seems to be
So many lonely people
Wonder why

Lonely man . . . lonely girl
I say a prayer for you
I pray . . . somehow
You'll see the sun
Shine through

Tomorrow
     Oh tomorrow
          No more sorrow
To see the sun shine
Beg . . . steal . . . or borrow

Red light/blue light
Swerving down
Six lanes of busy freeway
Smooth control
The traffic flow
For safety . . . down the way

Four boys lined up on the shoulder
Out on the town tonight
But they painted it
Just a little too red
Now four young faces
Are full of fright

Another night in the city
The many things I see
A thousand lonely people
Pass me by

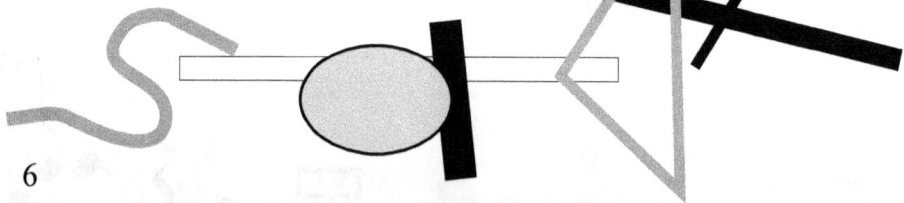

Another night on the freeway
The way it always seems to be
So many lonely people
Wonder why

Hurry people
On your way
Don't take the time to know
That even in the city
Flowers grow

Don't take the time to see
The sunset by the sea
The skyline
Or the moon that shines above me

Lonely boys . . . man . . . and girl
I say a prayer for you
I pray . . . somehow
You'll see the sun
Shine through

Tomorrow
    Oh tomorrow
        No more sorrow
To see the sun shine
Beg . . . steal . . . or borrow

State-Of-The-Art Moments

Images move around your life
Day and night
Zoom in and out
To delight you

Spark your senses
Feed on your desires
All designed . . .
To keep you hypnotized
　　Mesmerized

Colors
Images
State-of-the-art moments
　　Move you
　　Soothe you
　　Arouse you

Hypnotic effects
To keep you glued
The real
Made unreal
To keep you subdued

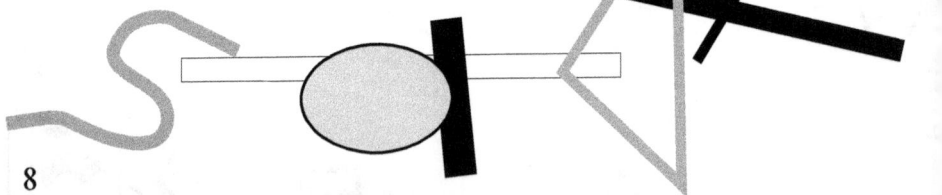

Can you break away
From all that vanity
Take some action
Get back . . . to humanity
Break the spell
    For your sanity

Colors
Images
State-of-the-art moments
    Move you
    Soothe you
    Arouse you

Hypnotic effects
To keep you glued
The real
Made unreal
To keep you subdued

As Far As We Can See

You know you come
From down below
From the poor side of town
You walk along with your crutch
While she's dancing
Free style

You think about how
The bad luck has been
While she gives you her smile
For free
. . . And you pass her by

But you could help her
With your common sense
Keep her from being raped
By this world of indifference

A world of indifference
Is where we are
A world of love
Is where we could be
If we could travel
    As far as we can see

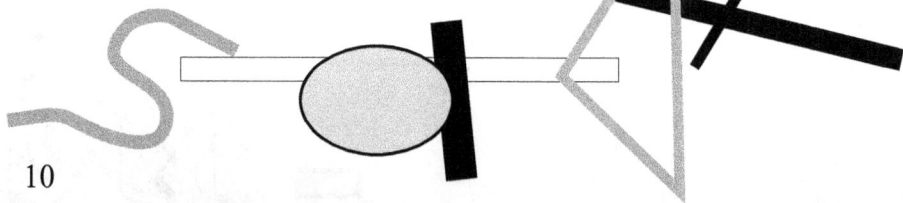

Things have come far
In such a short time
But people still live
In such different worlds
And yet they are
So close together

She is rich
And you are poor
She's used to money
You're used to the struggle
. . . As you pass her by

But you could help her
With your common sense
Keep her from being raped
By this world of difference

A world of difference
Is where we are
A world of love
Is where we could be
If we could travel
        As far as we can see

11

Is That YOU

Sometimes . . .
When I'm asleep at night
You materialize in my dreams
I see your hair
Your lips
Your eyes
Then like a cloud
You vaporize

I wonder . . .
Are you real

Are you the one
Who's like no other
Are you the one
Is that YOU

Are you the one
Who's like no other
Are you the one
Is that YOU

Sometimes . . .
I catch a glimpse of you
In the market
Or on the street
A hint of the glimmer
In your eye
Or a whisper
Of your smile

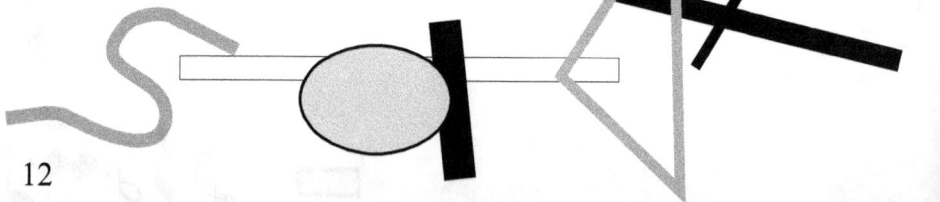

Where are you . . .
For real

Are you the one
Who's like no other
Are you the one
Is that YOU

Are you the one
Who's like no other
Are you the one
Is that YOU

Those secrets you hold
        Under cover
                Just for me

I wonder . . .
Where could you be

Are you the one
Who's like no other
Are you the one
Is that YOU

Are you the one
Who's like no other
Are you the one
Is that YOU

13

Morningstar

Be my Morningstar
I'll be your sunshine
Stay the way you are
This day will make you mine

The wind that blows you to me
Is a thing called Love
The teardrops that you drop on me
From up above

You are my cloud

Morningstar . . .
Shine for me
My life-giving rays
Will shine inside you

Morningstar . . .
By the sand and sea
You touch me
I touch you

You are the star
For which all evenings wait
Morningstar
Your love is my fate

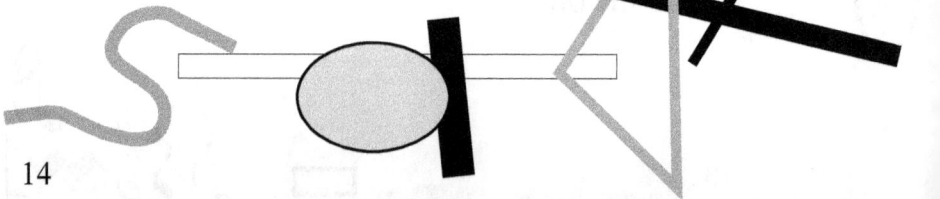

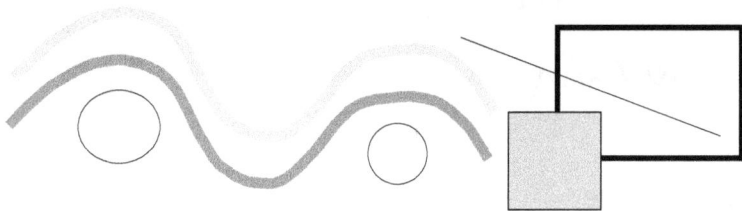

The warm sun rising
The air brilliant blue
The waves that are breaking
For just me and you

You are my Morningstar

Morningstar . . .
Shine for me
My life-giving rays
Will shine inside you

Morningstar . . .
By the sand and sea
You touch me
I touch you

Little Toy Gun

I gave you my name
And you gave me a son
He's starting to walk
I can't wait till he'll run

We'll ride him on ponies
He'll have lots of fun
But don't ever give him
A little toy gun

He'll go around shooting
You, me and a friend
But it won't be a *toy* gun
He'll use in the end

He'll find him a real one
In the armed forces
I don't want my son
Taking mass murder courses

So buy him creative things
Not for impression
Let him develop
His own self-expression

Expression is freedom
But don't get me wrong
I may not be free yet
But I'm getting strong

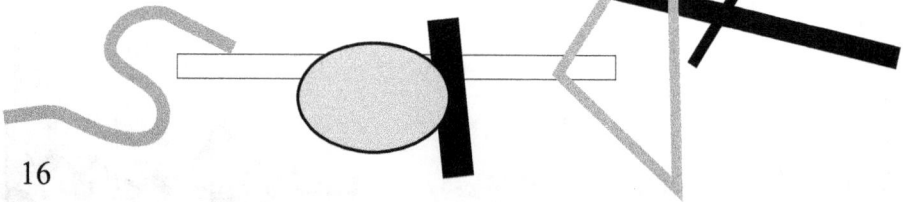

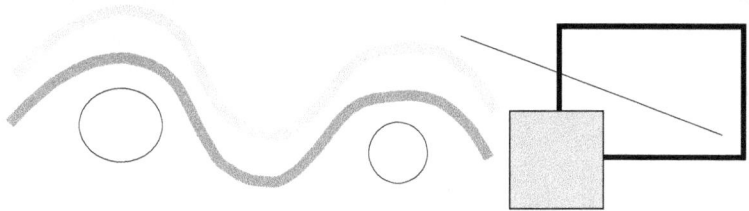

I have understanding
Of my own hang-ups
I need understanding
So I can be free

And then when our son
Needs someone to confide in
He always can come
To you, babe, or to me

Yes, I gave you my name
And you gave me a son
He's starting to walk
I can't wait till he'll run

We'll ride him on ponies
He'll have lots of fun
But don't ever give him
A little toy gun

Live And Learn

You say everything in the right way
And at the right time
And it's always all right in *your* mind
But it's the wrong time for lovin' you

I'm sorry for what has happened
I know sometimes I was wrong
Now all I've got is a song to sing
So let me sing it to you

You've got to live and learn
And when your whole world takes a turn
Don't let it hold you
Remember what I told you
I'll be there
        I'll be there

What does love bring
But hurt and sorrow
A good feeling today
A hope for tomorrow
But isn't it strange
How people change

I'm sorry for what has happened
I know sometimes I was wrong
Now all I've got is a song to sing
So won't you sing along

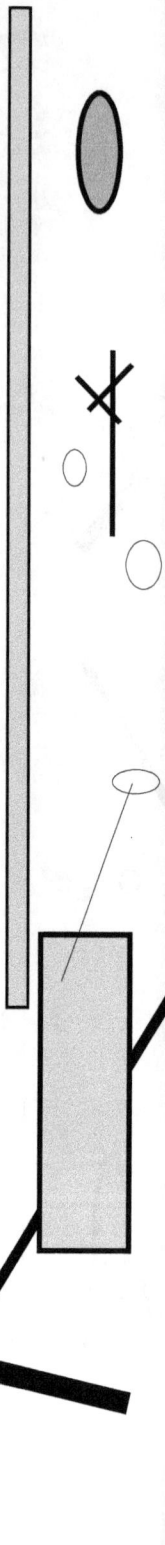

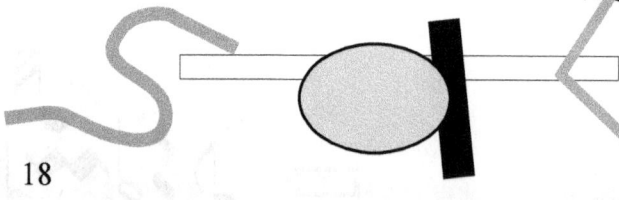

You've got to live and learn
And when your whole world takes a turn
Don't let it hold you
Remember what I told you
I'll be there
        I'll be there

I say everything in the wrong way
And always at the wrong time
But it's all right in *my* mind
It's just the wrong time for lovin' you

You've got to live and learn
And when your whole world takes a turn
Don't let it hold you
Remember what I told you
I'll be there
        I'll be there

A Little Bit Slick

Just a total distraction
    Painted feelings across your lips
Another chemical reaction
    Trickling down to my fingertips . . . but

Sometimes you're sweet
    Like a peppermint stick
A little bit spicy
    A little bit slick

Just another attraction
    Laying here across your bed
Another chain reaction
    Going off inside my head . . . but

Sometimes you're sweet
    Like a peppermint stick
A little bit spicy
    A little bit slick

Just a lack of traction
    Spinning wheels between your ears
Another emotional reaction
    Broken-down feelings behind my tears

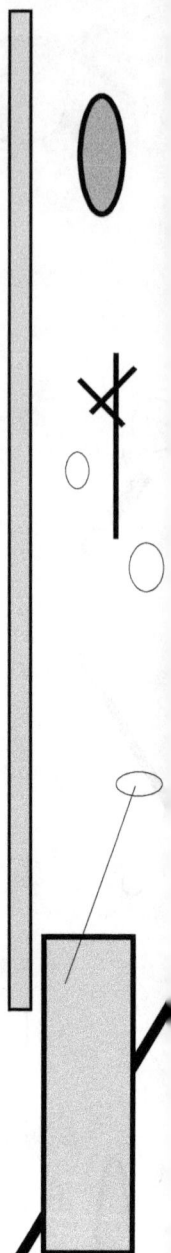

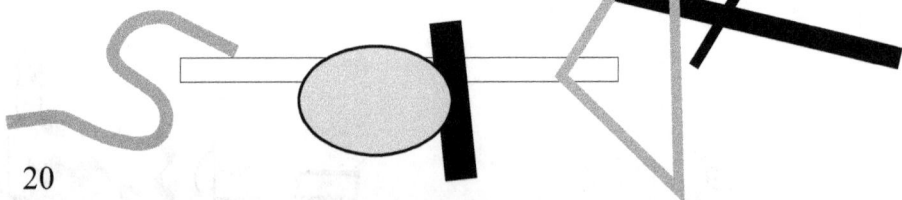

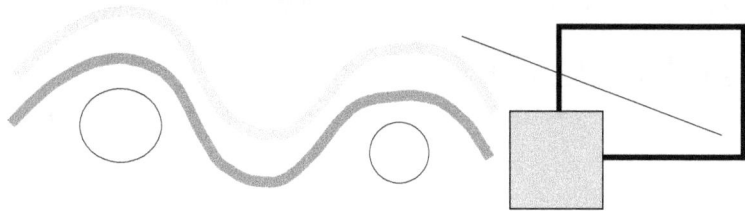

But . . .

Sometimes you're sweet
    Like a peppermint stick
A little bit spicy
    A little bit slick

Almost Made It

On the road to nowhere
I found your love
I thought it was the real one
They're always speakin' of

But sticky situations
Always follow you
And high-dramatic changes
You're always goin' through

Almost made it this time
Got so close
Could almost see it shine
Almost made it
Almost made it
This time

We almost made it
We almost made it
      This time

Now I'm not regretting
I ever knocked on your door
And I'm not forgetting
I always went back for more

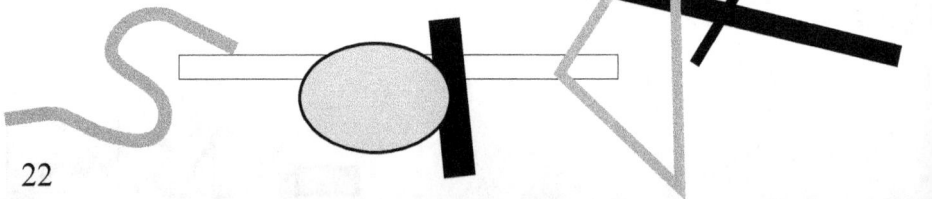

But I only wanted
For us to set love free
To feel its rhythm
And seek its center
        The secret center

Almost made it this time
Got so close
Could almost see it shine
Almost made it
Almost made it
This time

We almost made it
We almost made it
        This time

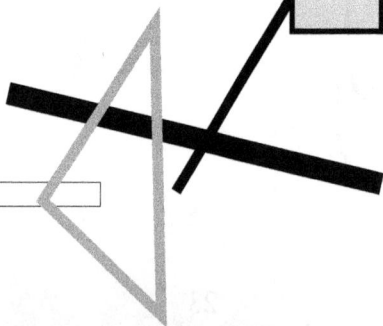

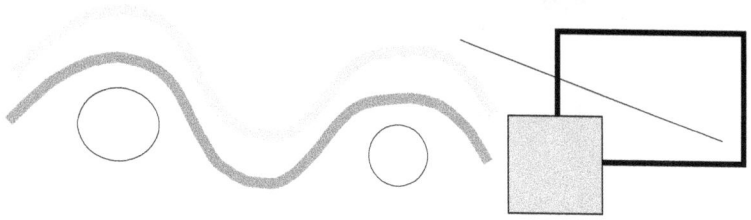

Side Two...

Lightning

Terra-firma . . . on the ground
Lightning striking all around
—Striking
In the night
Showing Her might

Tara-firma . . .
Coming home
I feel so alone

A song . . .
That's where I belong
What am I doing here
It's not so clear

In fact it's cloudy
All around
Lightning's striking
On the ground

It strikes so clear
And I wish you were near

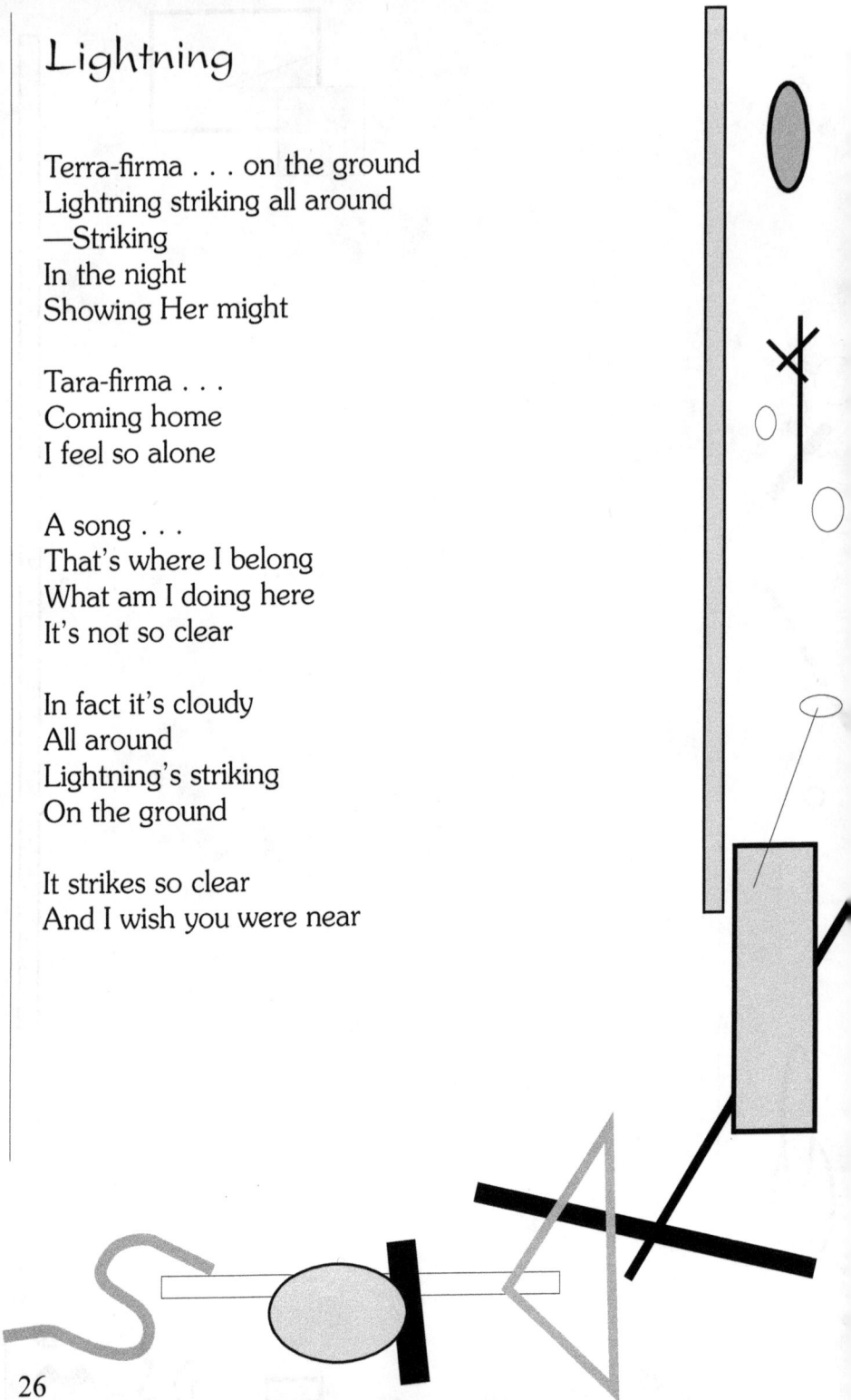

L
  I
    G
      H
     T
   N
    I
     N
      G

Piercing the night
—Striking
When it's right
Like a thousand stars
So bright
It strikes
With brilliant light
Fierce and bold
It seems so cold
Leaving you with chills
Imagine riding a lightning bolt
A thousand carnival thrills

It hasn't been my week
I'm thinking about what I seek
To be freely going
Where I was meant to be
Just trying to find the real me

I know where it is
But I don't have the time
Working so hard for a dime
But it's just like a song
    Or a dance
        Or a show
If you feel you are there
Then you know you can go

Looking out . . .
Through tornado skies
Lightning flashing
In my eyes

Show me the way
To get there . . . it's true
Show me the way
And I'll show you

L
  I
    G
      H
    T
  N
    I
      N
        G

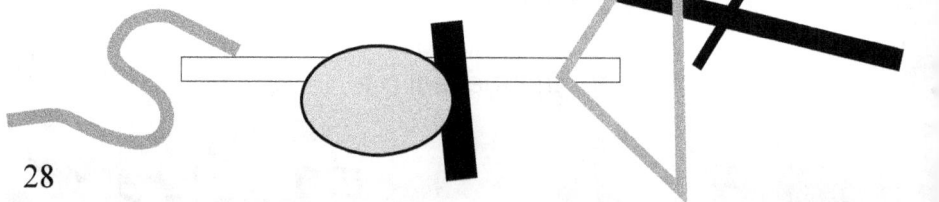

Piercing the night
—Striking
When it's right
Like a thousand stars
So bright
It strikes
With brilliant light
Fierce and bold
It seems so cold
Leaving you with chills
Imagine riding a lightning bolt
A thousand carnival thrills

Like an omen in the sky
You fly by
In my mind I can see
Where I long to be

It's close . . . you see
Not far away
Just trying to find
A better day

Tara-firma . . .
Coming home
I feel so alone
And there's—

L
 I
  G
   H
    T
   N
    I
     N
      G . .
          .
             .

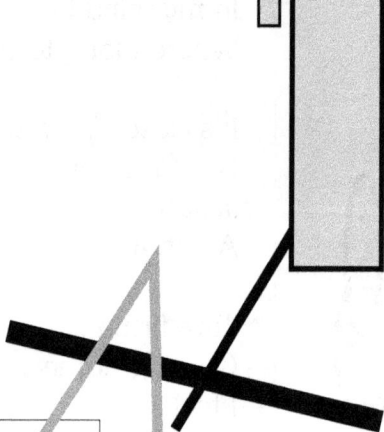

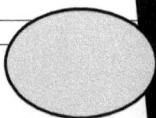

Rhythm

There still are some things
That are natural
Things which you cannot deny
Still some things
That can't be man-made
Like the sun, the trees and the sky

Through whispering canyons
Along waterfall lines
Searching for the wherefore and the why
If you want
You can close your eyes
But don't let the natural pass you by

And . . .
Rhythm . . . is something that's natural
Rhythm is something that's real
Rhythm is something you're born with
Rhythm is something you feel

You don't know how it comes out of you
You feel it comes from above
Rhythm is something inside of you
Rhythm is something like love

There are natural things
That you can find
No matter where you go
There is all the time
And all the places
To learn what there is to know

But in all these things
And all these places
Where do you find the glow
In your life
There is so much to do
And so many feelings to show

And . . .
Rhythm . . . is something that's natural
Rhythm is something that's real
Rhythm is something you're born with
Rhythm is something you feel

You don't know how it comes out of you
You feel it comes from above
Rhythm is something inside of you
Rhythm is something like love

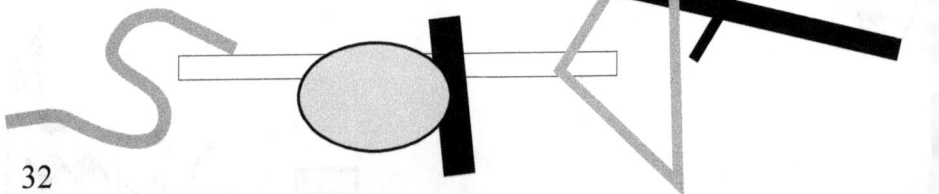

Oh, Big Sky

Oh, Big Sky . . .
Are you watching over me
Shall I say . . .
What I feel is real today

Will they listen to me now
Will it matter anyhow
What shall I do (for my soul)

    Do you think you are a master
    Do you practice what you preach
    So you think your way is faster
    Tell me . . . what is it you teach

    Do you show us how to love each other
    With more feeling everyday
    Are you helping anyone
    With more feeling . . . as you say

Oh, Inspiration . . .
Are you watching over me
Shall I say . . .
What I feel is real today

Will they listen to me now
Will it matter anyhow
What shall I do (for my soul)

If you want to start somewhere
Then start by being true
'Cause if you ain't true
Then we'll find somebody new

Now maybe you can help us all
With what it is you preach
But please don't say you know it all
There's always more to teach

Oh, Big Sky . . .
Are you watching over me
Shall I say . . .
What I feel is real today

Will they listen to me now
Will it matter anyhow
What shall I do (for my soul)

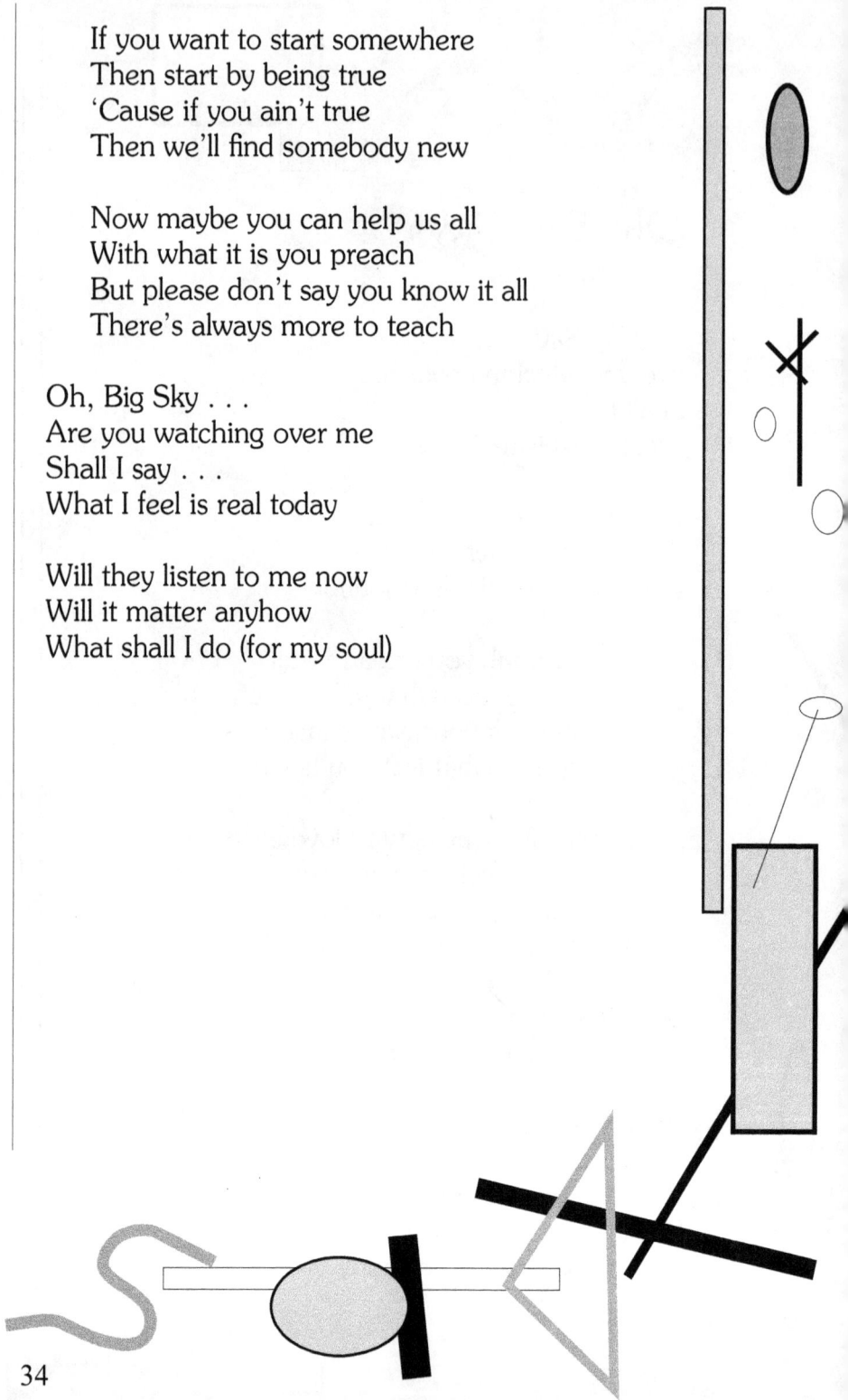

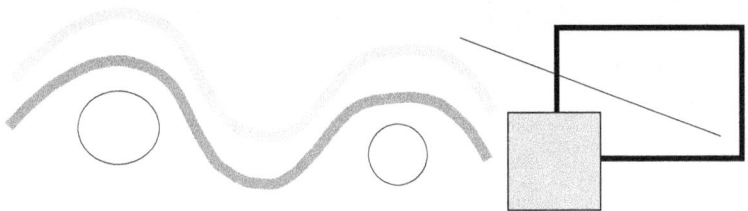

The Sunshine Shake-up

Wake up baby
      Wake up
It's time to hear from me

Wake up baby
Shape up
Climb down from that tree

Of dreams
And schemes
That someone's greed
Is puttin' on you

Don't you listen
Don't you heed
No more

Hear your heart—now
      Wake up
It's time . . .
For the sunshine shake-up

The sunshine shake-up
Is waking up the world
The sunshine shake-up
We're part of it . . . girl

35

The sunshine shake-up
Is shining through
The sunshine shake-up
Is coming after you

Wake up people
          Wake up
It's time to hear the call

Wake up people
Shape up
It's important to the future
Of us all

The greed that others
Are puttin' on you
It's time for compassion
To even the score

Hear your heart—now
          Wake up
It's time . . .
For the sunshine shake-up

The sunshine shake-up
It's waking up the world
The sunshine shake-up
We're part of it . . . girl

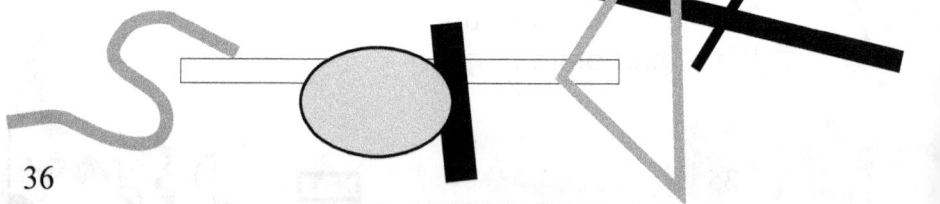

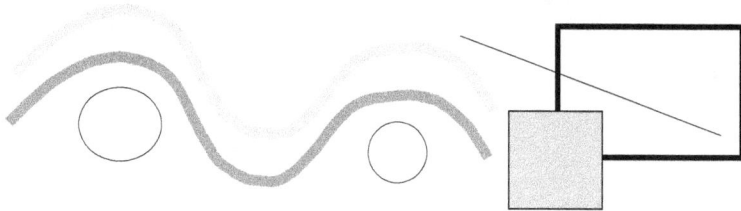

The sunshine shake-up
Is shining through
The sunshine shake-up
Is coming after you

Yeah . . .
The sunshine shake-up
It's waking up the world
The sunshine shake-up
We're part of it . . . girl

The sunshine shake-up
Is coming after you
It's time
For the sunshine shake-up

So . . .
Wake up!

She's Coming

For you and me
It's a time of trouble
Feast or famine
Wherever we go

It may sound simple
. . . Yes, it's true
But help your brothers
Is what you've got to do

That's still it—
Don't you know
The second coming
Will show

The second coming
Will be as a woman
Nurturing and compassion
Is what will show

It's got to be—
Don't you know
It's what we need . . . now
To grow

Higher . . . spiritually

Can't you see
All the waste we make
In our haste

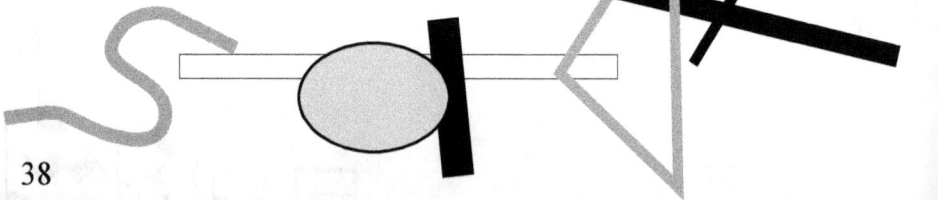

We leave behind
So much trash
To get there too fast

But where is it
We are going
Do you think you know

You may think
You're growing now
But the second coming
Will show

The second coming
Will be as a woman
Nurturing and compassion
Is what will show

It's got to be—
Don't you know
It's what we need . . . now
To grow

Higher . . . spiritually

Goddess of Love
Brings the Light
To shine on our needs

Coming soon—
To a state of mind
Near you

Dreams

Live your dreams
before they die
don't let anyone
tell you why you cannot

Just live them
for yourself
because soon enough
today becomes tomorrow

Dreams . . . dreams
oh, how you astound me
strange as it seems
I'm still full of dreams

Dreams . . . my dreams
are always around me
got to be true
to my dreams

If you don't
live your dreams
to the fullest
if you just
keep them inside
. . . put away

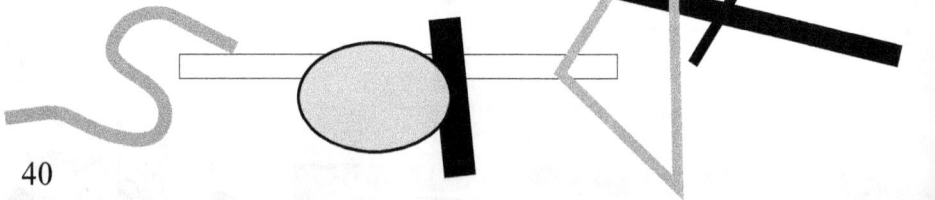

You'll just end up
          living
a life of longing
unfulfilled
never knowing
. . . the dreams of yesterday

Dreams . . . dreams
oh, how you astound me
strange as it seems
I'm still full of dreams

Dreams . . . my dreams
are always around me
got to be true
to my dreams

I thought that they
would go away
as I grew older
but no . . . still new
the dreams
dreams in me

The future
promises
dreams . . . for me
. . . for you
never stop
          dreams

Dreams . . . dreams
oh, how you astound me
strange as it seems
I'm still full of dreams

Dreams . . . my dreams
are always around me
got to be true
to my dreams

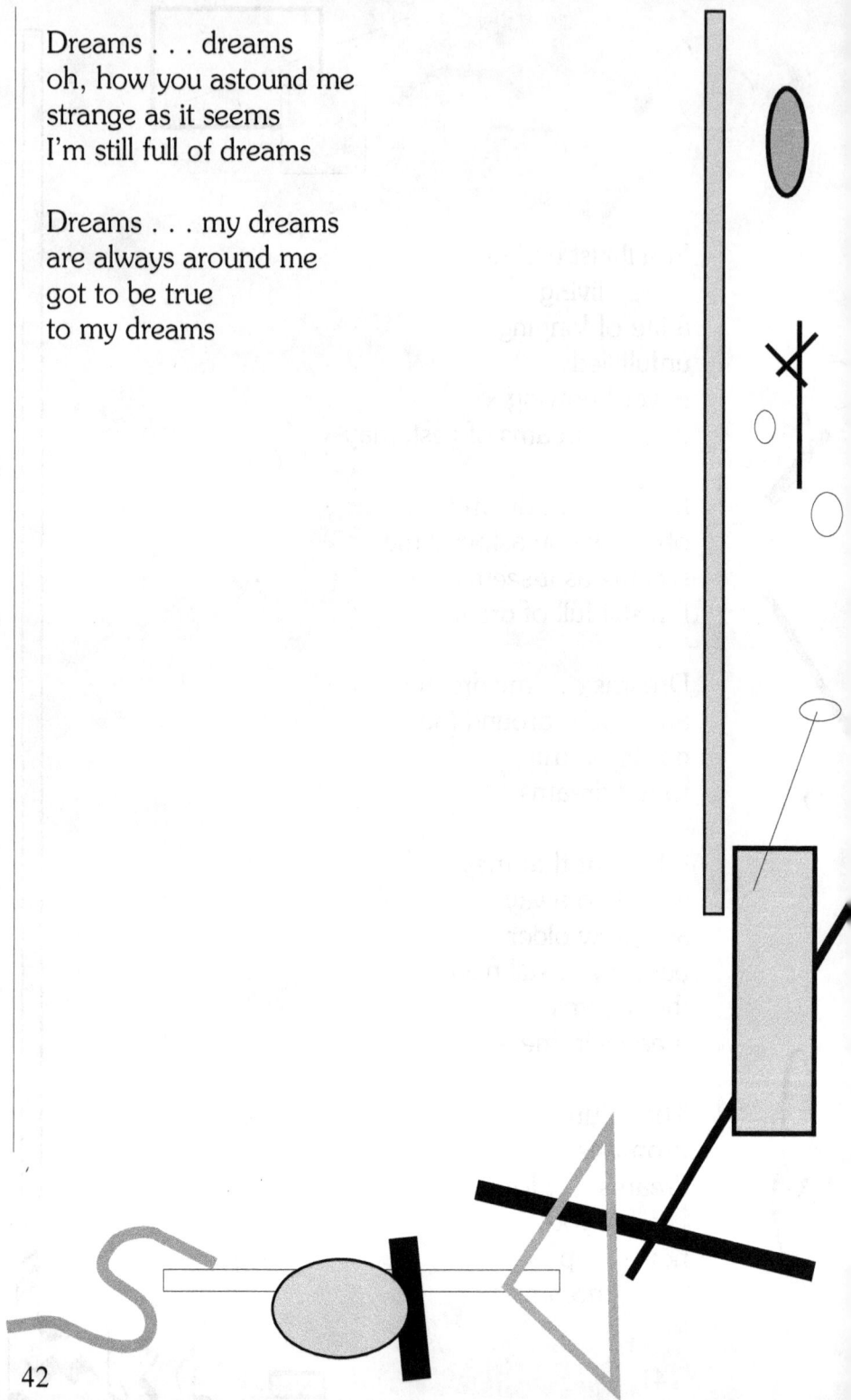

Promise What You May

Sunlight . . .
Bring my sunny day
Promise what you may
But come here along the way

I need . . .
Someone to hold me tight
To kiss me when it's right
And love me through the night

Riding in the breeze
        So free
Going just the way
I was meant to be

Yet I don't know where to go
To find that soft warm hand
Just trying to find some life
In this cold wasteland

In the city it's too noisy
I don't think my warmth is there
Everyone's just running
In a hurry to go nowhere

So I guess I'll hit the country
Just to see what I can see
Then maybe when the time is right
My warmth will come to me

Sunlight . . .
Bring my sunny day
Promise what you may
But come here along the way

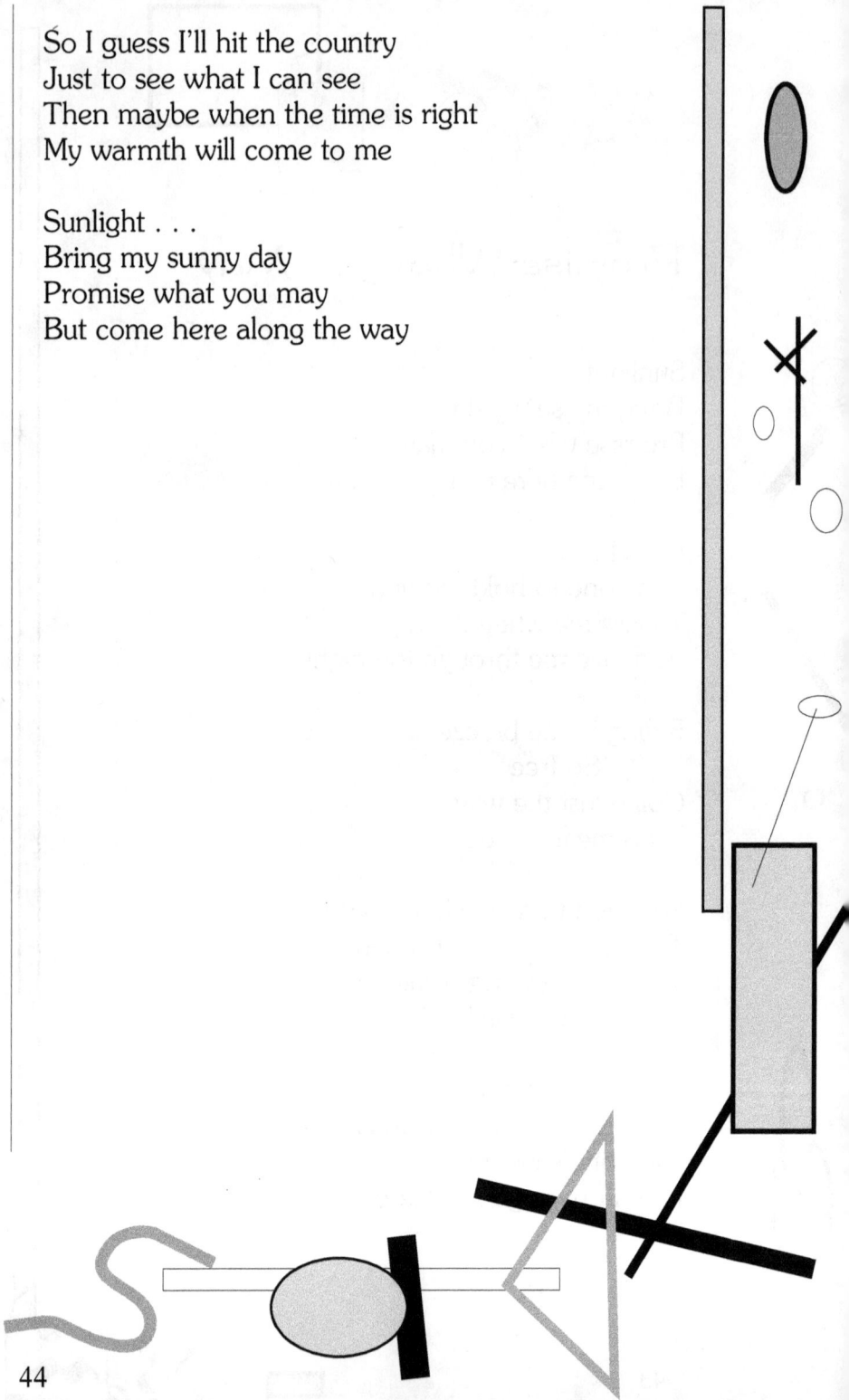

Strangers Turn To Fall

Sunshine in the springtime
Strangers turn to .

.

.

.

fall

Beckoned to the breaking summer
Follow true love's call

It's there for you
     For me
So much to do
     To see
True love sets you free
     Engulfs you blindly
       Undeniably

Writing up a storm
To quench the morning
     Greenery
The scenery of song
Directs the lover's long . . . long
     Yearning
For the knowing
     Of the glow

Of . . .

Sunshine in the springtime
Strangers turn to .

.

.

fall

Beckoned to the breaking summer
Follow true love's call

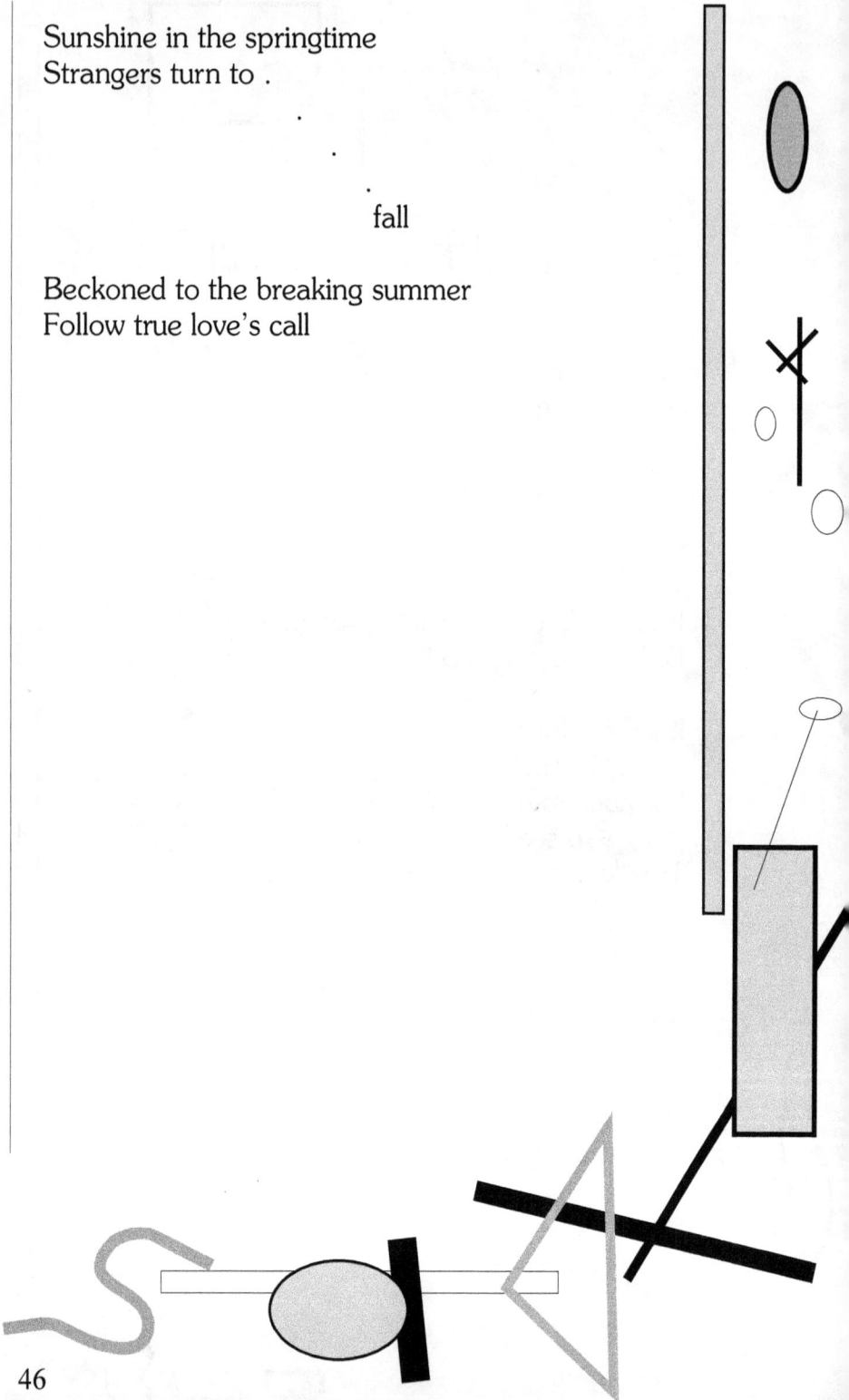

Got To Tell Somebody

I'd like to tell someone
What your love means to me
I couldn't make it nowhere
Without your love

Everything I do
Ain't nothin' without you
Don't you know how much
I depend on your love

All I ever wanted
Was for you to set me free
Just to hear you say
That's the way you want me

Now I don't know why
I feel this way inside
But it won't change
And I just can't hide it

Well I've got to tell somebody
I've got to tell someone
I've got to tell someone
About the love I've found

I've got to tell somebody
I've got to tell someone
I've got to tell the world
About the love I've found

With a little space
You know that love is free
You and I . . . girl
We have found the key

But when I come around
And you just can't be found
I think about how much
You mean to me

Well I've got to tell somebody
I've got to tell someone
I've got to tell someone
About the love I've found

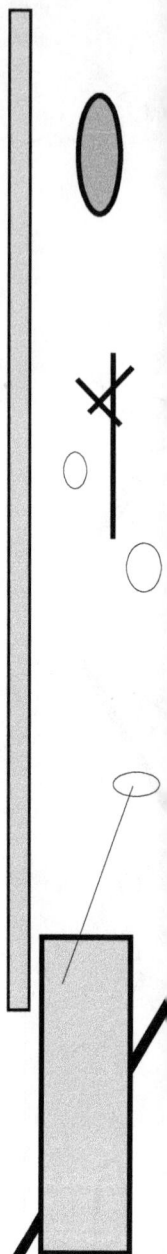

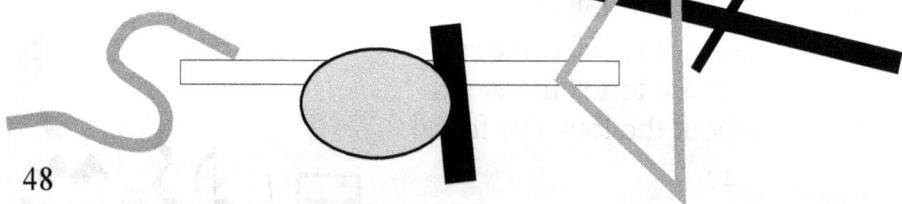

I've got to tell somebody
I've got to tell someone
I've got to tell the world
About the love I've found

Crying times are over babe
Now I know we can make it girl
I know we can . . .
We can go on
When love shows through

Well I've got to tell somebody
I've got to tell someone
I've got to tell someone
About the love I've found

I've got to tell somebody
I've got to tell someone
I've got to tell the world
About the love I've found

Yes . . . I've got to tell the world
About the love I've found

Yes . . . I've got to tell someone
About the love I've found

Yes . . . I've got to tell
 Woe . . . I've got to tell

 Yes . . . I've got to tell
 Woe . . . I've got to tell

 Yes . . . I've . . .
 Woe . . . I've . . .

 Yes . . . I've . . .
 Woe . . . I've . . .

 Yes . . .
 Woe . . .

 Yes . . .
 Woe . . .

49

I Was Always There

I was there
When you sang your songs
Dancing
Or just tagging along
Hoping
There was room for me
    . . . I was always there

I was there
For the harmony
Helped put it together
Whether two-part or three
You could always
Count on me
    . . . I was always there

I was there
For what it could be
There was always a vision
That I could see
Through it all
I heard the call
    . . . I was always there

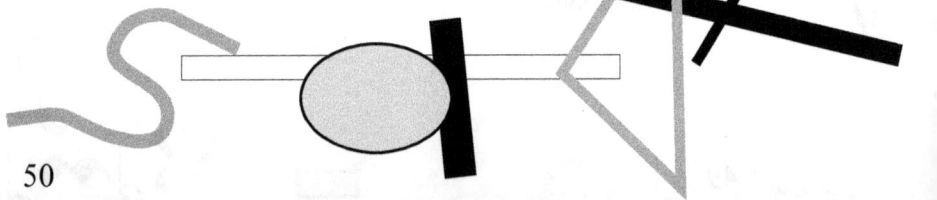

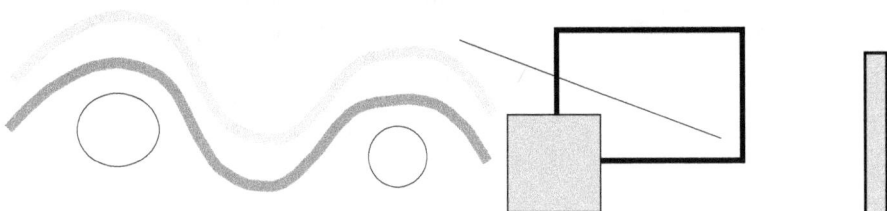

I was there
When you dreamed your dreams
Through the war
Even the heartache . . . it seems
I was there
Through so many things
. . . I was always there

I was there
For all your fame
And times
I even took the blame
And though
You didn't know my name
. . . I was always there

Index of original composition dates

About The Author

C. Steven Blue grew up in Los Angeles, California. He won his first poetry award at age 12, but did not start writing seriously until he was 18 (in 1968), when the tumultuous events of the 1960s, exploding all around him, inspired him to start writing poetry again.

After various jobs in his youth, Steven began a career in Hollywood stage production that lasted 27 years. He is now retired and living in Eugene, Oregon, where he pursues his poetry, publishing and performing, as well as producing and hosting local poetry events. All of these experiences have helped to shape Steven's poetry.

Throughout his life, Steven has also experimented in music and song-writing. Because of this, many of his poems are song-like. Steven has collected these works in a series of books called Wordsongs; each book containing 20 pieces, resembling a record album in scope and concept. We hope you have enjoyed this first book and will continue to read this unique series.

About The Symbols

PEACE BETWEEN MAN AND WOMAN

Steven designed this symbol in 1966 (at the age of 16) as a tribute to the Hippy idealism of the 1960s.

Now a registered trademark, it is both a valid and timely symbol for the third millennium.

AQUARIUS WITH LEO RISING

Steven also designed this personal symbol in 1966 as his own signature. His natal astrological sign is Aquarius, with Leo rising, represented here by the Sun (Leo's ruler) rising over the symbol of Aquarius.

About The Artwork

All of the computer graphics, symbols, pictures and illustrations in this book were created by C. Steven Blue. All photographs are owned by C. Steven Blue.

MORE BOOKS

BY

C. STEVEN BLUE

S.O.S. ~ Songs Of Sobriety ~
A Personal Journey Of Recovery

WILDWEED

Black Tights — Poetry X

Published by

ARROWCLOUD
PRESS

For more information go to www.wordsongs.com